The Compassionate Cats

The Gatos of Spain

By

Beverley B. Starr

ISBN: 1-4107-3206-1 (e-book)
ISBN: 1-4107-3207-X (Paperback)

This book is printed on acid free paper.

1stBooks - rev. 5/19/03

The Fascinating Cat

Never underestimate a cat
They are clean, intelligent,
Friendly, beautiful and
Mysterious.

You can't own a cat.
They alone decide where
They will live and who
They will love.

Dedicated to:

My Children,

Gene, Libbie and Chester

And my 11 grandchildren

With all my love

Mom

PROLOGUE

It was a clear day in Salamanca, Spain. From my sixth floor window, I could see the arch with the inscription over the gate to the hospital, across the street. It read, "Hospital Santisma Trinidad"; Residencia "Stma Trinidad"; "Tercera Edad". A high wall extended from the gate and enclosed the grounds and building. The location of my room enabled me to see over the wall into the courtyard, and the activity, which caught my attention this day, was the family of gatos (cats). There were nine all black and white, and they looked to be playing follow the leader. The leader was negro (black) and muy grande (very large). Later I learned his name was Pablo and that he was the father of the family.

On this day he led them to a three-foot high wall where he sat; the rest sat below him on the ground, and looked up at him as though they were at a meeting. They sat there for about fifteen minutes before leaving.

After this I spent quite a lot of time watching the gatos. Not being used to napping in the afternoon, I found it hard to fill the time, while everyone else was taking a siesta, from two-thirty until four-thirty every afternoon. This is when I took up my position at my window and watched the gatos.

I was visiting Spain and attending school each morning to study Spanish. I lived with a Señora Calista in her apartment, which was directly across the calle (street) from the wing of the hospital, which housed the old people and the courtyard where the gato family lived. I learned a lot about the patients and the gato family during the six weeks I was there. This is their story.

The Cats

Pablo, the padre (father) of the gatos, is from a town called Zamora. When he was young his human owners took him on a trip to Salamanca. They went shopping and left Pablo in the coche (car). Being curious, as all cats are, Pablo decided to take a walk and look around. When he returned to where the coche had been parked, it was gone. This didn't bother Pablo much because during his walk he had seen a lovely blanco gato (white cat). He decided to go back to where he had seen her. Flor (flower) was beautiful and all blanco (white) except for a black spot on her left side, which was shaped, like a flower. It was love at first sight for both of them. Flor lived at the hospital, and she took Pablo back to live there too.

1

Flor and Pablo named their first kittens, Shan, Skit and Sophie. Flor said she liked the sound of S's. When their next kittens arrived, she named them Sleer, Sumi, and Sissy; finally there was little Sookie the baby. Shan and Skit are twins, both Negro and very much like their father. They help him to catch mice around the hospital. This they feel is their job since they live on the grounds. As Pablo says, "Everyone must earn their way."

Sophie is the oldest girl gato; she has a black spot on both right legs and the rest of her is blanco (white). She is very lady like, gentle and sweet, like her mama. She helps her mama by keeping the younger girl gatos in line and teaching them to behave.

Sissy is a free spirit who is very curious and ends up getting into trouble a lot of the time.

She is blanco with dos (two) negro spots on her back.

Sumi is a very quiet and lady like gato. She and Sissy are nothing alike even though they are the same age. Sumi is white except for a tiny black heart on her back. Pablo wanted to name her Lovely, but Flor said no. She felt all of the kittens were lovely and it wasn't right to call only one of them lovely.

Sleer is the same age as Sissy and Sumi but looks like his father and brothers, all shiny and black. When he grows up he will be as muy grande as they are. In his manners he is more like his sister Sissy, curious and always getting into trouble.

Sookie is the baby of the family; she is black like her padre but tiny and very dainty, soft and sweet natured.

One of the wings of the hospital is a nursing home where doce (twelve) old people live. At the time of this story there were seis (six) señores (men) and seis señoras (ladies).

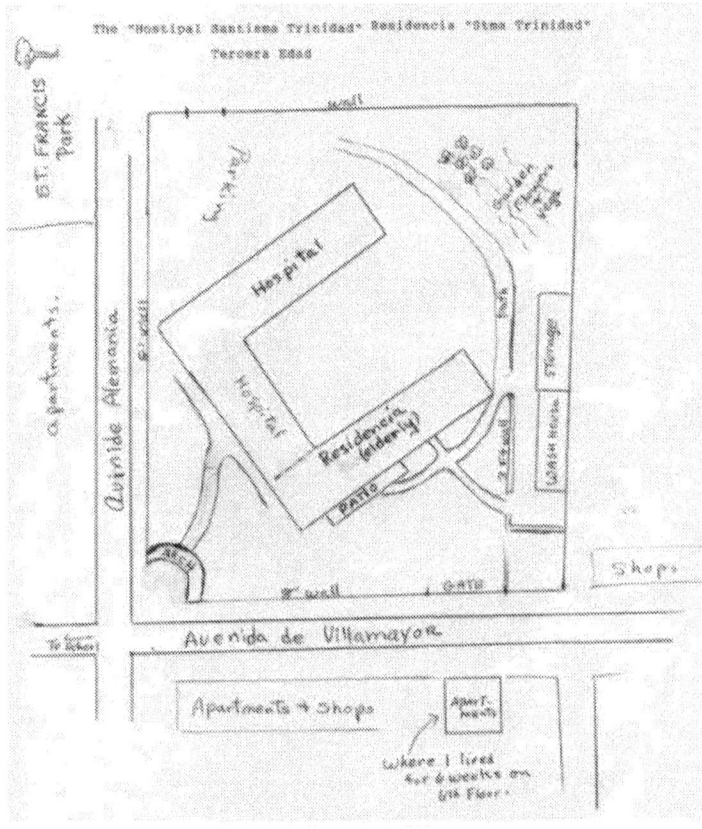

Doctor
Sáinz

Head of Hospital
and
Nursing Home

With nine gatos around, one can only assume that the good Dr. Sainz is fond of gatos.

Head Nurse
NURSE
Concha
with Flor

Concha is the head nurse for the nursing home. She is a pretty Spanish lady, who lost her husband after three years of marriage. The nursing home is her life and she enjoys working with the patients and she is a super nurse.

NURSE
CONNIE

Connie is a slim dark-haired girl who became a nurse so she could meet a doctor and marry. She is a good nurse, but doesn't like to work at the residencia because she doesn't get to meet any young doctors. She would rather work at the hospital, but until there is an opening, for another nurse, she has to stay at the residencia. She likes working with the patients, but she really wants to meet her doctor.

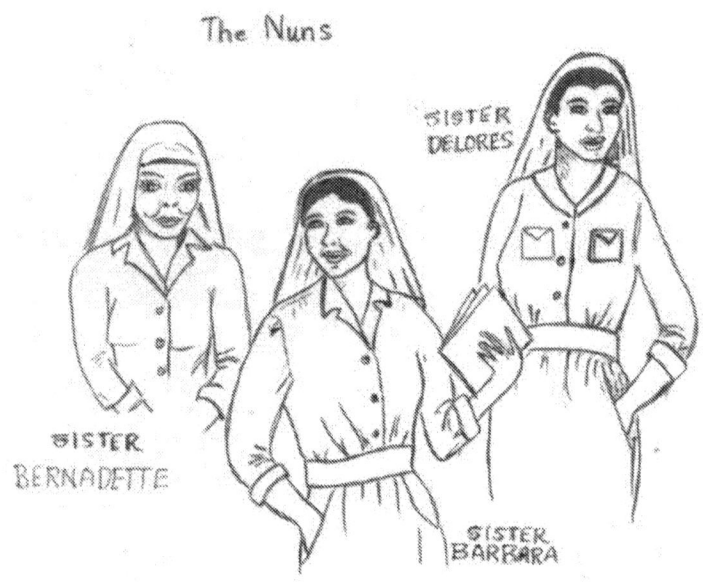

The Nuns

Sister Bernadette is the daughter of Jerome and she works in the Hospital, which is connected to the nursing home. She is friendly with Sister Barbara who works with the old people. They are both nursing sisters and belong to the same religious order.

Sister Delores also works with the old people. She loves cats. They love her also. She saves them nice tidbits, which the patients leave on their trays. She is sweet and gentle with the old people and they all love her.

Doctor Mark
TAPIA

Dr. Mark is the grandson of Oliver Tapia. He finds much more than a job when he visits his grandfather.

PEDRO LOZANO
Gardener/
Handyman

Sookie

Pedro is the handyman and gardener for the hospital and grounds. He is old himself but not old enough to live at the home without working. He has two more years before he will be. He is a friend with the gatos.

ANDRES BENET
Orderly

Andres is the orderly who helps the nurses with the heavy lifting and other work at the nursing home. He is about forty and a college graduate but finds his job very satisfying.

VALDES ANDVES

LAWYER

Valdes is the son of Francisco. He has two reasons for helping with a birthday party his father and a certain pretty head nurse.

Beverley B. Starr

The Residents

Mattie Nó - 80
& Sophie

16

First there is Mattie, who is eighty years old. She has four children. Since they all have their families, she feels it's better for her not to live with any of them. One of them visits her once month and they take her home on family birthdays, most of the time, and at Christmas, Easter and some other special occasions.

Isidoro 90

sumi

Isidoro is an independent, feisty old lady of
ninety and is still spry for her age. She slips

outside often, and goes out on the street, wanting to go shopping. Once, she managed to get three blocks away, before she was found and returned to the hospital. She promises each time, she won't leave again, but she forgets and off she goes again. She has a daughter who lives in Paris, France. The daughter writes a duty letter once a month but never comes to visit her mother.

Isabel Gasco
86

Ana Civieta
83

SLEER

Isabel is eighty-six and is mixed-up. She thinks she is Queen Isabel and that Ferdinand is her king. She keeps telling everyone that when Colombo returns he will bring her gold, silk and spices for India. She wears a tiara and always says, "We wish to go out" or "We wish to eat". She has a sister Ana whom she thinks is her lady-in-waiting, and she refuses to be told anything different. Ana can't walk very much as she has gout.

Teresa 78
and Sissy

Then there's Teresa, who is seventy-eight. She can't see very well so she doesn't walk around much since she gets lost very easily.

She sits in her room and is very lonely. Sometimes a sister or nurse thinks of taking her to the dayroom or patio. She has gotten to be rather timid and shy since losing much of her eyesight.

Teresa hasn't any family except an older brother who left for America many years ago. She hasn't heard from him in almost twenty years.

Marie Alonzo-82 & Flor

Marie is a very tiny lady who is eighty-two. She was an actress when she was younger and sometimes forgets, and thinks she is still on the stage. She still puts on makeup and dresses up more than any of the other patients. She loves to talk about the parts she has played and the plays she was in and how beautiful the costumes were. She has no visitors and she is lonely.

The men at the nursing home are as different as the ladies.

Oliver Tapia-80

There is Oliver Tapia, eighty years of age, who likes Mattie very much. He is too shy to tell her so he just takes walks with her. Sometimes Oliver will pick a flower, during their walk, and give it to Mattie, who takes it to her room and puts it in a vase. She likes Oliver a lot and sometimes she will put her hand on his arm while they are walking. She also saves her cookie at lunch to give to him, because he loves sweets. Oliver has a grandson, Mark, a newly qualified doctor.

Jose Marcos
96

Jose is the oldest person living at the
nursing home. He's ninety-six. He has no

living relatives. He can neither see nor hear very well, and only leaves his room when someone has time to help him into a wheelchair and pushes him out to the patio or dayroom. He is able to eat his meals by himself but often he knocks over his milk.

Francisco
Andṽes

89

Francisco is eighty-nine. It happens; his birthday is the same day as Luis's. They will both be ninety in just a month. Luis' son, Valdes, visits his father every couple of weeks. Most often on Sundays, he takes him out for Chinese food. It is his favorite meal. Valdes knows about his father's birthday being the same day as Luis's birthday, because Sister Bernadette told him.

CARLOS CALVO, SR.
83

Carlos is eighty-three with no family. He thinks Marie is the most beautiful little lady he has ever seen. He is always watching her and sits beside her whenever he has the chance. He thinks she is wonderful.

Luis is eighty-nine; he has a son who's a big politician. Luis stays in a wheelchair due to a stroke a few years ago. He is a very lonely not having seen his son in three years. He feels no one loves him or cares.

He wonders why he can't just die and be with his Mary. Mary was his first and only love and they were married for fifty-six years before she died.

Jerome Piñel 81
Sister Bernardette

Jerome who is eighty-one has seven daughters, all except Bernadette the youngest, are married with families. Bernadette is a nun and she works at the hospital. She tries to see her father every day if she isn't too busy. The other six girls come to see their father two or three times a year, because they say that Bernadette is there if daddy needs anything, Bernadette will take care of it. They forget to write most of the time. Jerome tries not to mind although it does make him sad. He tries not to let Bernadette see how sad he is.

The Gatos get Involved

One day in early summer the gatos were lying in the sun, on the walk in front of a wall, where the wind couldn't hit them. They were dozing, because it was a lazy sort of day. Sister Barbara and Nurse Connie were walking past the washhouse to get some clean linen. They were talking. Sister Barbara was saying it was a shame that Luis was feeling so down because his son never comes to visit him. Connie said she wished she could tell the son how terrible he was, not visiting his father, and that he should be ashamed of himself. Sister Barbara said she had an idea that might make him come to visit. She told Connie that Luis and Francisco would both be ninety years old on the same day. If they had a birthday party on the twenty-ninth of June, which was their birthday, and invited the press and television, to cover it, then the son, being a politician, would have to come. Connie thought it was a great idea and said she would talk to head nurse Concha. But Sister Barbara said, "No! Talk to Sister Bernadette and ask her to talk to head nurse Concha, there's a better chance of her agreeing." When Sister Bernadette was asked, she suggested she talk to Señor Valdes, Francisco's son, who was a lawyer, and let him suggest it to Concha, this would be even better. When Señor Valdes talked to Concha he offered to help make the arrangements such as ordering and paying for the birthday cakes, and contacting the families of the patients as well as the newspaper and the television station. Head nurse Concha thought it was a great idea and that it might help the patients to feel a lot better if they had a party and their families.

She got the permission she needed and gave Señor Valdes the names and addresses of the families of the patients. Now Señor Valdes did not know that Luis Rojos, Jr. had stayed away from his father because he was ashamed that his father was in the residencia and that if people knew, it might ruin his political career. When he called Luis, Jr., and requested his help, after telling his about the newspaper and television, Luis, Jr. had to agree to help.

Flor liked to know what was going on and ever since the gatos had overheard Nurse Connie and Sister Barbara talking, she had wondered if they were really going to have a party. She wasn't sure what a party was but it sounded like something she wanted to know about. Flor decided to lie down on the windowsill of the office and pretend to be asleep and listen. It did not take her long to realize there was a lot going on other than a party. She told the gato family that evening, the nurses and doctors were worried about the patients, because their blood pressures were too high, they were not eating, and they were sad and cranky, and lonely. No one seemed to know what to do for the anciano la gente (old people).

Flor sighed as she finished telling her family about the old people. Sookie, the bebe (baby) gato said, "Why can't we go see them and cheer them up? We could do it! They are always calling me and they like to hold me and pet me." The other la muchacha gatos (girl cats) thought it was a great idea, but the boy gatos didn't like the idea. This is how the gatos started to visit the anciano la gente (the old people). At first they only went onto the patio and porch and let the old people hold them on their laps. Then after awhile the old people would hide them under their lap robes or shawls whenever a nurse or doctor came around. Sometimes they even carried them back to their rooms.

One day about a week later, Flor was at the vantage position pretending to sleep as usual, when she heard head nurse Concha telling Sister Delores that the patients seemed to be happier and eating better but she didn't know why they were happier, because none of them had even had a visitor. Sister Delores said, "Have you noticed that every one of the patients have had lower blood pressure readings for several days?" They couldn't figure out why the change but were pleased anyway. Flor thought she knew and went to talk to her family.

After listening to the girl gatos tell of their experiences, the boy gatos began to feel left out of the fun. They decided to visit the patients also.

The residencia was becoming a cheerful place. The nurses were puzzled at the change in the patients, but the old people were not telling. They were extra careful in hiding the gatos. The conspiracy was bringing the old people together; making them friendlier to each other and making them feel less lonely.

Teresa Dominguez and Sleer

Teresa was tired of sitting in her room. She hadn't seen anyone since they had cleaned her room after breakfast, a couple of hours ago. She was thinking of when she was poco (little) and how happy she and her brother had been with their parents. There was the day when they were playing in the hayloft and Juan told her that someday he was going to America. He told her all about what he had read about America. She remembered about when he had hugged and kissed her goodbye and promised to write from America. His letters stopped coming after a few years. When their parents died in a fire, which destroyed their home, she wasn't able to get in touch with him to tell him. Several years later she married and moved to Salamanca. She hadn't heard from her brother in many, many years. She couldn't remember how many but she still thought about him and wished she knew if he were alive and where he was so she could write to him. She felt alone and tired of life and the tears rolled down her cheeks.

Suddenly Teresa felt a presence and she quickly brushed the tears away but not before Sleer saw them. Sleer walked over to her chair, very straight with his tail nicely curved up over his back; put his front paws up on her chair and his chin against her leg. Teresa reached out and patted Sleer's head. Sleer jumped lightly onto her lap and lay there purring contently. Teresa stroked Sleer behind his ears and gradually forgot to be lonely. Sleer felt warm and purred. Teresa felt the purring which seemed so friendly. She suddenly felt content and happier than she had been in a long time. She had a new friend. Every day Sleer would come to see her and lay on her lap. Teresa began to look forward to his visits. Sometimes Sleer would see her out on the patio and visit her for a while. Teresa began to have an appetite and she began to spend more and more time away from her room and began talking to the other patients.

Mattie No` and Sophie

Mattie knew it had been her choice to come to the residencia to live, but she sometimes wished that one of her children had cared enough to insist that she live with them. When Señor No` was alive, she had her own home and she was happy. Her el hijos (sons) and hijas (daughters) and their children were in and out all the time. They had made a schedule and they came one at a time as though it were a duty instead of out of love for her. She missed sitting around the table drinking café (coffee) and everyone talking.

Yes, Mattie had to admit she was lonely. She missed her niños (children) she mustn't think of them as niños for they were all grown now and had niños of their own. She did enjoy holidays when they came and got her and took her home with them and they all got together with all their niños. When she had to come back to the residencia she did miss them all so much. Yesterday she had spent the day with Alice, her oldest daughter, as it was Alice's birthday. Ever since they had brought her back to the residencia, she had felt like crying. She was trying so hard right now, not to cry, but her heart ached so much. Just at that moment Sophie came by and sensed that Mattie need company, so she jumps onto the arm of the chair and steps onto Mattie's lap and reaches up and kisses Mattie on her cheek. Mattie pats Sophie and it makes both of them feel better. Mattie suddenly decides she should stop feeling sorry for herself and at about that time Oliver walks by. Sophie jumps down and rubs against Oliver's leg and he stops, and when he does, he sees Mattie. Mattie smiles and he smiles back and she asks him how he is and he says he feels great. By this time he is sitting in the chair next to Mattie and Sophie gets back into Mattie's lap and purrs and purrs while Oliver and Mattie hablo and hablo (talk and talk).

Oliver Tapia and Sophie

Oliver had always been shy ever since he was a small child. He had been intending to speak to Mattie but whenever he got close he couldn't make himself stop and speak. He hadn't got up nerve to stop until Sophie stopped him. Somehow Sophie gave him the courage to look at Mattie and when she smiled, he smiled and suddenly everything was easy. Gatos were great and Mattie seemed to think so too.

Oliver was wondering why he was afraid to speak to Mattie because it was really easy to talk to her and she liked to talk about the same things that interested him. They talked about their families. Oliver told her that his only living relative was his grandson Mark who was twenty-eight. Mark, Jr. looked just like his father looked when he was young. Mark had just finished up his intern and residency and was a full-fledged doctor. Oliver was bursting with pride of his grandson. Mark wrote to his grandfather often. He wasn't married because he had wanted to finish his schooling first and get settled. Oliver was looking forward to calling him Dr. Mark Tapia, M.D. He was hoping that Mark would get a practice close enough where he could see him often. Mattie told him to pray about it and God would take care of everything. Mattie suggested that they walk down to the chapel right then and they did. Sophie went off to get her lunch and she was very satisfied.

Jerome Piñel and Skit

Jerome has seven daughters, Ana, Bernadette, Colixta, Delores, Elizabeth, Florence and Glorida. All of them married well except Bernadette who wanted to become a nun. All the girls kept so busy with their social lives that they put off writing or visiting with the father. Only when their conscience bothered them did they make any effort to come to visit or to write. Two or three times a year was about as often as any of them came to visit Jerome. Each of them thought, "Bernadette is there. She will see that he is alright." Jerome loved all of his daughters but Bernadette held a special place in his heart.

Jerome is almost bald, he has a little fringe around the bottom and he is short and chubby and tries to keep a smile on his face so that no one will know how sad he is that none of his other six daughters come to visit. He hadn't seen any of them except Bernadette for the last four months. He didn't know how they or their families were. He knew he should be thankful he had so much family when some of the patients had no one at all right at the moment though he felt all alone. He was sitting by the window in his room and thinking about the past, when the girls were young and his darling wife Mary was still alive, and how happy he was when he came home from work to his eight beautiful ladies. No he felt he couldn't bear it, the way things were.

Skit had been watching all morning to see whom he could visit and whom he could cheer up. He wasn't sure what he was supposed to look for or what to do when he found it. He and his twin Shan had always just caught mice, but since all the mice had been caught, there wasn't anything to do. Pablo, their padre, told them they should help cheer up the old people. Skit wasn't used to being inside the building where the old people lived and he was nervous, so he was lying on the windowsill of Jerome's room. He had dozed when he heard a noise. Jerome was blowing his nose and wiping his eyes. Skit felt real sorry for him and went to Jerome and sat looking up at him and purring. Jerome looked down and spoke and patted his lap. Skit decided Jerome wanted him to jump up onto his lap, so he did. Jerome started to rub Skit behind his ears and boy, did it feel good. Jerome talked to him and told him all about his wife and daughters and how happy they had been when they had all been together. Finally they both dozed off and didn't wake up until the dinner bell rang. Skit left to get his own dinner before the nurse came in and found him in Jerome's room and chased him out. Jerome told him to please come to visit him again and Skit kissed him on both cheeks to let him know that he would come back.

Skit thought that the girl gatos were right. Visiting the patients was really fun and made one feel good and important. He couldn't wait to get back to see if Shan had found it as exciting as he had.

Marie Alonso and Carlos Calvo
Flor and Sookie

Marie is a tiny little lady and still very pretty. She has lovely gray hair and still uses makeup and loves to wear pretty clothes. She gets mixed up sometimes and thinks she is still an actress. She never has visitors as she has no family and no friends, so she is a very lonely lady living in the past. She remembers when she was a star and the plays she starred in. She sometimes gets confused and thinks she is the person whom she played in the part of in a play. It's so confusing to remember what is real and what is make believe.

Marie loves to talk but there is no one to talk to. She likes to sit on the patio because it's up from the ground and she feels as if she is on the stage again. Every morning she sits on the patio until lunchtime. Today she is sitting and dreaming of the past and the leading men she had acted with, when Sookie came along and decided to meet the pretty lady. She rubs up against Marie's leg and Marie reaches down and picks Sookie up and puts her in her lap. Sookie loves this, and purrs and purrs, delighting Marie. Marie tells her about a play she was in, in which she had a cat and told her about the costumes and some of the lines she had. Marie finally had someone to talk to.

Marie was so busy talking to Sookie that she did not notice when Carlos came and sat in the chair next to her, nor did she see Flor come up to Carlos or Carlos pick up Flor. Not until Carlos said, "I saw that play and you were wonderful as the princess and so beautiful and you're still beautiful." Marie was so surprised to find Carlos sitting there and asked, "How long have you been sitting there?"

He said, "Oh, a little while, I didn't want to disturb you because I was remembering the same as you and enjoying it too! I hope you don't mind."

"No, I don't," she said. "Did you ever see any of my other plays?"

"I've seen every play you were in, and I've liked you in all of them." He said. They talked on and on and Sookie and Flor went to find someone else to cheer up. They knew Marie and Carlos would keep each other company.

Carlos had been walking in the garden when he saw Marie on the patio with Sookie. He really liked Marie, as he had seen all her plays and had imagined himself in love with her when he was younger. He really wanted to know her better, He was too awed to speak to her, even though he often sat next to her and tried to think of something to say.

Flor had been looking for Sookie and had just happened by. She thought maybe she would give Carlos courage to speak if she helped. She and Sookie were both satisfied as they left.

Luis Rojos and Shan

Luis is eighty-nine and wishes he were dead. He doesn't understand why God has let him live so long. His Mary has been gone for fourteen years and he still misses her so much. His son is ashamed that he is in a nursing home. He doesn't want his father living with him because he is a big politician, and he and his wife, Mable entertain a lot, and the old man would be in the way. He doesn't visit his father for fear someone would see him and find out. Frankly, Luis Rojos, Jr. is a snob of the worst sort. He hasn't been to see his father in three years.

Luis is in a wheelchair and he can move himself slowly, but is unable to walk since his stoke left his legs very weak. Luis is very sad today and not interested in anything. The nurse has just left him sitting in the warm sunshine on the patio right by the long bench where Shan was lying. When Shan saw the nurse coming he jumped off the bench and hid under the bench until after she left. Then Shan jumped back onto the bench and sat and looked at Luis. He could tell something was wrong because Luis didn't seem to notice him. Shan watched for a while and finally ventured to put a paw on Luis's arm Luis didn't notice. Shan patted his arm a few times and at last Luis noticed him, and said, "Well, hello there little gato. Did you come to cheer me up?" Luis reached out and patted Shan who stepped over onto Luis's lap because Luis was having trouble reaching him. Luis talked to him and Shan answered with nice comforting purrs. That is the way they spent the morning on the patio until they heard the nurse retuning for

Luis, to take him to lunch. Shan jumped down and hid under the bench again. After they had gone Shan went to find Skit and see how he had spent the morning. Shan had enjoyed being with Luis and hoped he could see him every day.

Isidoro Alvarez and Sumi, Sissy and Pablo

Isisoro was feeling lonely today because she had received a letter from her daughter in Paris. She was trying to remember just how long it had been since she had seen her. "Let's see, I've been here five years and she hasn't been to see me since she brought me here. I remember her saying, 'Mama, it's real nice here and I'll come to see you often.' She had written a few times but there is always some reason she couldn't come to visit. She always says, 'Maybe I can come next month.'"

Sybil, her daughter was married and had one daughter.

Isidoro had not seen her granddaughter since she was fifteen.

Isidoro decided she should go shopping and buy her daughter and granddaughter some presents. She could send them and then maybe they would come to see her. Being very independent, she decides to go right then without telling anyone. She walks down the drive without meeting anyone, and when she gets to the gate, she decides to sit on the bench there and rest and get her breath.

While Isidoro is sitting there, Sissy and Sumi see her and realize that she is about to leave the hospital grounds. While Sumi goes to find Pablo, Sissy goes to Isidoro, to try to keep her from leaving. Sissy sits right in front of Isidoro and purrs real loud and Isidoro speaks to her and picks a flower growing by the bench. Sissy pretends to smell it then backs away, then smells it again and backs up again, trying to make Isidoro forget that she was going to leave the grounds. Finally Pablo arrives. Pablo and Sissy decide to put on a show for Isidoro. Sissy lies down and Pablo jumps over her then he lies down and Sissy jumps over him. By this time Isidoro is laughing at them. Then Andres arrives, with Sumi leading him, and he sits beside Isidoro and watches for a few minutes before he tells Isidoro that it is time for lunch and takes her by her arm and walks back up the drive to the residencia with her. Pablo, Sissy and Sumi go to get their lunch as well.

Isabel and Ana

Isabel woke up and she decides she wants breakfast in bed. She claps her hands together to call her lady-in-waiting. Then she pushes the button to call the nurse.

Nurse Connie comes in with a bright smile and says, "Buenos días (good morning) Isabel, how are you this morning?"

Isabel snaps at her, "Don't you know you should curtsy to me young lady? I'm your queen."

Connie says, "Now, now, Isabel, you know better than that. Here let me fluff you pillow."

"Don't you dare to touch me, you silly creature, get my lady-in-waiting immediately! I won't have you here. Do you understand? Get out! Now!" About this time, Ana comes into the room to see about her sister and she tells the nurse that she will handle Isabel.

Ana says, "Buenos Días Isabel, here's you juice. After you drink it, I'll help you get dressed. It's a lovely day. We can go out on the patio and sit in the sun for awhile." All the time Ana was talking, she was helping Isabel to dress and she didn't stop talking for a minute because she didn't want Isabel to start thinking she was a queen again. She never stopped until she got Isabel seated in a rocking chair on the patio.

Ana is eighty-three. She is often disgusted with Isabel and says to her, "Sister, do shut up and stop acting a fool." Isabel doesn't pay any attention. Ana then says to anyone around, "don't pay attention to her, she's crazy." Whenever Isabel feels too ill to get up, Ana hovers over her as if she really is a queen.

She's afraid of being alone if anything happens to Isabel.

Now Sissy had decided to stay around the patio to see who she could visit this morning. When Isabel and Ana came out and sat down, Sissy thought Ana looked like she was the nicest but thought she would sit and listen for awhile to make sure. Isabel and Ana sat and talked and talked and Sissy closed her eyes for just a minute and went fast asleep.

Party Plans and Dr. Mark is Hired

One morning, head nurse, Concha, Nurse Connie, and Sisters Barbara and Delores were discussing the patients and the party plans. As usual, Flor was lying on the windowsill pretending to be asleep, but really listening. Later Flor told the rest of the gatos what she had heard; Luis Rajos' son had promised to come to the party. Actually he had promised to help with the arrangements.

Isidoro's daughter Sybil and her granddaughter, Edith was coming from Paris. Of course Francisco's son, Valdes, would be there since he was organizing all the arrangements for the party. Mattie's children were all coming as well as Jerome's daughters and their families.

Mark, Oliver's grandson, had been invited when he stopped by to see his grandfather. Oliver was so proud. He introduced him to everyone. When Dr. Sāinz came to see Oliver while Mark was there, he asked Mark where he planned to practice. When Mark told him he would like to practice near by so he could see Oliver often, Dr. Sāinz told him to go to see the Chief of Staff at the hospital and tell him that he had sent him. Dr. Sāinz said there was an opening for another doctor at the hospital. Mark went right away and applied for the job and was hired right then.

The birthday party was to be held on Saturday, June twenty-ninth, which was the day of Luis and Francisco's ninetieth birthday.

The gatos all hoped they would get to be at the party too, because they had never been to a party and it sounded exciting.

All the patients except Luis and Francisco knew there was to be a surprise party for Luis and Francisco. They were all very careful not to mention the party. Mattie, Isidoro and Jerome did not know that their families had been invited, so they also were to have a surprise.

The gatos were visiting every day and the patients were happier and the nurses still didn't know that the gatos were the reason for the improvement in the patients. The patients were careful to put their lap robes or sweaters over the gatos whenever they saw a nurse or doctor coming.

Flor was kept busy trying to keep up with all that was going on. She spent more and more time on the office windowsill. She was reluctant to leave for fear she would miss something important.

The Mystery

Pedros, the gardener would give Sookie a flower, which she would take in her mouth and she would take it to one of the patients. Nurse Connie noticed that all the patients suddenly had a flower in their water glass on their bedside table. Connie asked Mattie who had brought her the flower and Mattie just smiled and said, "A dear friend brought it." So Connie asked Marie and Oliver where their flowers came from and they both just smiled and, "A dear friend brought it." Later Connie and Concha were talking about where the flowers could have come from. Concha said that there hadn't been any visitors except Sister Bernadette in over a week. When Sister Bernadette was asked about the flowers, she said, that she would ask her father where his flower came from. Jerome just smiled and said, "Why daughter, a very sweet friend brought it to me." Bernadette asked who the friend was. Jerome said, "A very pretty young female." That was all Bernadette could get out of Jerome. None of the nurses had seen any visitors to the patients.

Flor listened to the nurses talking and wondering about the flowers; finally she left and went to find her family so she could tell them how Sookie had managed to fool all the nurses.

As far as the patients were concerned they were enjoying themselves and they would gather together on the patio and visit with each other, and tell how the nurses tried to get them to tell about the visitor who was bringing flowers, whom the nurses had never seen. The patients all vowed never to let anyone know their secret about the flowers or the gatos.

Another Mystery

Dr. Mark and Dr. Sāinz were making rounds in the nursing wing of the hospital. Dr. Mark remarked that he had never seen such happy and contented patients in a nursing home before. He asked Dr. Sāinz what they were doing different from other nursing homes. Dr. Sāinz said he didn't know of anything different being done. In fact a couple of weeks before all the patients had been depressed, lonely, fretful, not eating and unhappy. 'I don't know what has caused the change," he said. That afternoon Dr. Sāinz called a staff meeting of the workers and nurses in the elderly wing. Dr. Sāinz said the change of atmosphere and the outlook of the elderly patients in the nursing wing impressed him. He asked how it had come about. The nurses said they didn't know. They went on to tell him about the mysterious appearance of the flowers and the visitor that the patients insisted had brought them, whom no one else had seen. Dr. Sāinz asked if the patients had been eating okay. Head nurse Concha said, "For the last week everyone had been cleaning their plates when before that they were barely touching their food." Dr. Sāinz said that there had to be a reason for the change since whatever it was affected all the patients. He also requested that everyone keep their eyes and ears open and see if they could discover what was going on.

Unfortunately, Flor wasn't present at this meeting so the gatos were not aware that the patients were going to be watched closer. The gatos got a little careless in their comings and goings.

Concha's Discovery

Concha saw Sookie with a flower in her mouth and watched her while she gave it to Isabel. Then a little later she saw Shan lying on Luis's lap and when Luis saw her coming, he put his lap robe over Shan. When she was giving out medicine she saw a white gato tail sticking out from under Mattie's robe. She knew now what had changed the patients. She decided that for the time being she would keep quiet. She loved cats and as long as the patients were happy and so contented she didn't see who it could hurt. Connie too had seen a couple of the gatos with Oliver and Francisco from a distance but by the time she got closer a lap robe had covered them up. So she too decided to keep quiet.

Connie and Dr. Mark were seeing a lot of each other when they were off duty. Connie thought that at last she had found her doctor. She was so happy she couldn't bear to tell on the gatos when they were bringing so much joy to the patients.

An Engagement

On Friday, the twenty-eighth of June, Connie and Dr. Mark had a dinner date. After dinner they went to St. Francis' Park, which was across the avenida from the hospital. It was there that Dr. Mark told Connie that he loved her and asked her to be his wife. He gave her a beautiful ring and they decided to announce their engagement at the party the next day. Dr. Mark went to tell his grandfather first and Nurse Connie called her parents, who were happy for her and asked that the young couple come to let them meet Dr. Mark as soon as they could arrange their schedules.

The Day of the Party

Saturday, June twenty-ninth was a beautiful day from the moment the sun came up. The party was to start at eleven o'clock in the morning since the families of the patients were coming from some distance. It would give everyone lots of time to visit before lunch, which was at two-thirty and the big meal of the day.

Isidoro cried when Sybil, her daughter arrived. Sybil's daughter and her husband, whom Isidoro had never met hugged her and kissed her. Isidoro couldn't stop hugging and kissing her daughter. Isidoro kept saying, "I can't believe you've finally came."

Mattie was surprised to see all four of her children with their husbands and wives and their niños (children). They invited Teresa to sit and visit with them. Theresa was glad since she didn't have any family

Luis just couldn't believe it when his son, Luis, Jr. and Mabel his daughter-in-law arrived. They had never visited Luis since he had come to live at the nursing home, but here he was – and Mabel had come too. He wondered why they had come, since they had never come before. He had forgotten that it was his ninetieth birthday, until Luis, Jr. Hugged him and said, "Happy Birthday Papa." Luis cried and Luis, Jr. cried too and said, "Oh Papa I'm so sorry that I haven't come to see you before. Forgive me Papa, I love you."

Francisco woke up knowing that this was his ninetieth birthday and he was expecting Valdes today. Valdes came often but it wasn't only just to see his papa. He was also interested in Concha. He had managed to find out that she was thirty-three years old and a widow. He liked the way she looked and her smile. He wanted to know her better, much better.

Valdes had come early so he could help with last minute things that needed to be done for the dinner and the party afterwards. Concha had the day off but had promised to help Valdes. She enjoyed being with him. He laughed a lot and made everything fun.

The T.V. people were expected at one-thirty and there were a lot of loose ends to tie up. Valdes had hired people to decorate and others to cater special dishes for dinner. Microphones needed to be checked and the musicians shown where to setup their combo. It looked like it was going to be a great party. Valdes got things started and then went to see his father and wish him a Happy Birthday. The party was to be a surprise for Francisco and Luis so he didn't mention the party.

Jerome was really amazed when two vans drove up and his six daughters with their husbands and children piled out. It had been too long since the whole family was together. It was wonderful. Tears came to his eyes, he was so happy. They all gathered around Jerome, hugging and kissing, laughing and talking. It was a beautiful and wonderful day for Jerome.

By two-thirty everyone had caught up on all his or her family news. Ana and Isabel had been asked to join Mattie's family. Isabel forgot to pretend to be a queen, which pleased Ana. They all went into dinner when the dinner bell sounded. Ana puzzled about the change in Isabel and she meant to ask her about it later.

The young girls who were fascinated by her stories of when she was an actress surrounded Marie. Of course Carlos was there also urging her on by saying, "Tell them about when you played Camilla. You were so beautiful."

A couple of Jerome's grandsons stayed with Jose and very carefully pushed his wheelchair, which made them feel very important. They would talk about Jose and the wheelchair for weeks afterwards.

So, no one was left to feel lonely. Everyone was surrounded with love on this special day.

The dining room was decorated with colored streamers and blue and yellow balloons, yellow tablecloths and flowers on every table. With all the patients, doctors, nurses, the Bishop and special officials, T.V. people and hospital personnel, there were about one hundred or more guests.

Dr. Sāinz asked the Bishop to say grace, then they all sang happy birthday twice, once for each birthday person.

A delicious dinner was served and then two big birthday cakes were brought out, each had one big candle. It would have been too many to put ninety candles on each cake. Everyone had a slice of cake.

Dr. Sāinz introduced the special guest and then Dr. Mark. He said that starting immediately Dr. Mark would be in charge of the residencia part of the hospital. Dr. Mark was very surprised and he thanked Dr. Sāinz and said he had been doing a little research about the recent improvement of the patients High blood pressures being lowered, less depression, better appetites were some of the improvements. "It seems we have some unpaid help and I believe they are here today. Ladies and gentlemen please remove you lap robes and shawls from our gato family. Pablo, Flor and their family, Sophie, Shan, Skit, Sissy, Sleer, and Sookie, from now on you are welcome to visit the patients. You won't have to hide any longer. We wish to thank you for what you have done for our patients." Everyone applauded.

"I have two other announcements to make. Mattie and Oliver plan to marry and they have asked to remain here. Permission has been given. Also Nurse Connie has consented to become my wife. You are all invited to the wedding, which will be held in the hospital chapel next month. You will be sent an invitation. I want to thank each of you for coming today and want to remind you how much your visits mean to our patients. Now Sister Delores has a few words to say to you."

Sister Delores got up and said, "I have a letter here, which I have been asked to read to you."

The Letter

Dear Friend or relative;

I am here because I am old. Time has run out on my usefulness. The quality of my life doesn't matter to my family or the few friends left. Every day I sit and wait. I wait for a visit, for a touch or a sign that I am remembered. My greatest fear is that the people I love have forgotten me. I have nothing to look forward to, so I live in my memories of all my yesterdays. The present is too full of hurt and loneliness and pain. I am weak now and I don't fit into your life style. I have been put away like a book which as been read and put on a shelf, forgotten and left to gather dust. But I am not a book. I have feelings. I have lived too long. Now I'm weak, I hurt, I cry, I'm lonely, so I retreat into the past when I was strong and useful and happy. You discuss me as though I'm deaf or not present. I can hear you. You say I'm senile, but it's only my way of coping and escaping from my loneliness and hurt. I'm sorry if this letter upsets you but it's something I've wanted to say to you for a long time, but have been unable to. You don't listen because you don't want to hear. I guess that's you way of coping.

I understand and I still love you as I always have.

Just a patient at Santisma Trinidad Residencia.

When Sister Delores finished there were few dry eyes and people were blowing their noses and wiping their eyes. Many family members put their arms around their loved ones and there were promises that things would be different in the future.

Mattie's children were very surprised to hear of her coming marriage to Oliver. Her two daughters promised to take her shopping and buy her a wedding dress. They decided they would get married the morning of the same day that Mark and Connie would get married in the afternoon. This way everyone could attend both weddings during the same trip.

There were promises of returning for the weddings.

The band played and everyone visited, and at last it was time for the guests to leave. After all the guests were gone, the nurses began to get their patients back to their rooms and get their patients settled for the night. They were satisfied there were no lonely patients at Santisma Trinidad Residencia that evening and the future looked very bright indeed.

Jose Dies

The day after the big party dawned clear. Everyone was content and happy. The nurses started on their morning rounds, checking temperatures and blood pressure on each patient. Things were not to remain cheerful for long though.

When Nurse Concha went into Jose Marco's room he appeared to be still asleep, but when she went closer she found that Jose had passed away in his sleep.

She summoned Dr. Mark, who came quickly. He asked Nurse Concha to call Dr. Sāinz; since he didn't know what the hospital's procedure was when there was a death. Dr. Sāinz explained what needed to be done.

Since Jose had no living family having outlived all his relatives at ninety-six, the hospital would have to make funeral arrangements.

The coroner came and gave them permission to make funeral and burial arrangements.

The hospital chaplain arranged for the funeral to be held the following day in the chapel. It was agreed that any of the patients in the residencia who wanted to should be allowed to attend. To try to keep the death a secret would upset the patients. They would miss Jose and also it would be impossible to keep such a secret.

Nurse Concha went to the patients and told them of Jose's death and that they could attend his funeral in the chapel if they wished to. All the patients said they wanted to attend.

Sister Bernadette took the flowers from the party and she rearranged them and put them in the Chapel for Jose.

After the funeral, the patients returned to the residencia part of the hospital. The hearse came and took Jose to the cemetery, where he was buried, with only the chaplain, Dr. Mark, Dr. Sāinz, and Nurse Concha in attendance.

Back to Normal

For the rest of the week everything was calm. The daily routine returned to normal, with the gatos freely visiting the patients. While the patients were pleased and happy to have the gatos around they thought it wasn't as much fun as when they were putting the gatos visits over on the nurses. Sookie continued to bring the patients flowers but it wasn't the same.

Mattie and Oliver were often seen sitting next to each other and holding hands. Sophie was always with them. She felt very proud that she was the one who got Mattie and Oliver together. They belonged to her, and all the other gatos knew it.

Ever since the party there were more visitors. Family members dropped by whenever they were near doing their shopping.

While it made more work for the nurses, they didn't mind, because the patients were thriving health wise. Also, the entire residencia was a cheerful and happy place.

Sister Barbara said, "I can't believe the change from a couple of weeks ago. The patients were depressed and this whole place was lethargic and dismal. Now we are all bouncing around. Blood pressures are down and appetites are up."

Sister Delores replied, "I agree, but you know there seems to be more gatos around since they are out in the open. Do you think they know that they don't need to hide from us anymore?"

"I don't know, but they have really made a big difference. There are a lot more friendly smiles now," answered Sister Barbara.

Beverley B. Starr

The Shopping Trip

As promised, Mattie's two daughters made arrangements to take Mattie shopping for a dress to be married in. Meanwhile, Mattie has been thinking whether she wants a long dress or a short dress and what color she would like it to be. She decides to ask Oliver his favorite color. Oliver thinks about it and says, "A pretty blue, kind of a medium blue, not too dark and not too light."

Finally the day comes when her daughters arrive to take Mattie shopping. They tell Nurse Concha that they will be gone all day. Nurse Concha said, "Be sure to take some rest periods so your mother won't get too tired."

"Don't worry, we will," said the girls.

Mattie tells her girls, "What I would like is a soft blue dress that is long enough to reach half ways between my knees and my ankles. I would like it to be soft, full and swirly."

They visit many dress shops but not one has what Mattie wants. They finally stop for lunch before returning to shop. A few hours later they find a shop, which has a dress that seems right. When Mattie tries it on it is too large and Mattie gets upset but the sales lady tells her that it isn't so big that it can't easily be altered to fit. Mattie calms down and the sales lady pins the dress where it's needed and tells them it will be ready for them in three days.

A couple of doors down the street they find a shoe store where they find some shoes that will go with the dress. They stop at a sidewalk café and have a cup of tea before going back to the coche to drive back to the hospital where they tell the nurses on duty that their shopping trip was a success. They had gotten the perfect dress for Mattie.

Connie said, "I have to go shopping to get my wedding dress. I'm off tomorrow, so I will go then."

Connie wasn't able to go shopping or even get her day off.

Some of the patients became very ill during the night with food poisoning and for several days all the nurses had to work extra hours to take care of all the patients.

Connie's Wedding Dress

After the birthday party where Dr. Mark had announced Connie's and his marriage plans, they decided they needed to tell their families also. First they called Connie's parents. Mark talked to Connie's father first and asked for his permission to marry his daughter. Then Connie talked to her father and after that they both talked to her mother. They told them that they were planning the wedding for the thirtieth of the next month. Her mother promised they would come and that they were very happy for them.

After hanging up they called Mark's parents and told them the happy news, inviting them to the wedding. Mark asked his father if he would stand up with him as his best man. His father said, he would be proud to.

Connie still had not been able to shop for a wedding dress. The other nurses were helping address wedding invitations and were talking about Connie taking the next day off to shop for the dress. A deliveryman came into the office with a big package. He needed a signature. He said it was for Nurse Connie Pando. Connie signed for it. When she opened the package there was a beautiful ivory satin wedding dress. They all gasped at how lovely the dress was. There was a note from her mother, which she read.

"To my dearest darling daughter,

Your father and I are so happy for you. We will be there for your wedding. We will come early so I can help you dress. I am sending you this wedding dress, which I hope you will wear. Your grandmother wore it when she married your grandfather, forty-six years ago. I wore it when I married your father, twenty-eight years ago. It would please both your grandmother and I if you will wear it when you marry Mark. Our marriages have been very happy and we want your marriage to be happy too. We have always considered the dress had a certain magic, which we hope will pass on to you and Mark.

With all my love,
Your mother

P.S. Your grandmother will be coming with us.

Connie cried. She was so happy she couldn't help it.

She said, "It's the most beautiful dress I have ever seen. It's perfect and just what I wanted." She tried it on, after closing the door, and it was a perfect fit. The other nurses thought it was wonderful and said so.

All she needed to shop for now was some shoes to match.

The wedding dress, which Connie's mother sent, was Ivory satin with a cathedral length train. It was an embroidered Italian gown trimmed with Viennese lace and had long romantic sleeves, which ended in a point over her hand. The veil was also of Viennese lace and fell below her waist. A band with pink rose buds attached held the veil. She would wear ivory satin shoes and planned to carry a nosegay of pink rose buds and white baby breath.

Mattie's Wedding Dress

Mattie's wedding dress was soft blue chiffon, which swirled around her calves. The bodice was beaded with small pearl beads. There was a long sleeved lace jacket and a small cap with dainty net and tiny white flowers to wear on her head. Low heeled shoes dyed to match complete her outfit. She planned to carry a bouquet of white roses.

Her oldest daughter brought her a string of pearls, which had been given to Mattie by her first husband on their wedding day, and Mattie had given them to her oldest daughter when she had gotten married. Now her daughter was returning them for Mattie to wear again when she married Oliver. Mattie wasn't sure that it was a good idea for her to wear them. Her daughters insisted that it was all right for her to wear them, but Mattie just wasn't sure.

When Mattie's daughters came several days later they brought the altered dress and the shoes which had been dyed to match the same shade of blue as the dress. They also brought the tiny cap with all its frill of net and tiny white flowers. Mattie tried everything on and it all fit and looked just fine. She still had doubts about the pearls but the girls finally persuaded her that it was all right to wear them.

Who is Juan Miguel?

Valdes was sitting in his law office when his secretary buzzed him and told him that a Mr. Miguel was there and wished to see him. Valdes wasn't busy at the time so he said, "Send him in please." He got up and met Mr. Miguel at the door. He told him to have a seat. Mr. Miguel looked to be about eighty.

Valdes said, "Mr. Miguel, how may I help you?"

Mr. Miguel answered, "I would like to hire you to find my sister. I have searched for her for years. I arrived a few months ago from America where I hired many private investigators to search for her. None of them have been able to find her. I am getting old and I'm running out of time. My name is Juan Miguel I'm eighty-two years old and my sister is seventy-eight, if she is still alive. Before I die, I would like to find her. Money is no object, as I am very rich. Will you help me?"

Valdes said, "Mr. Miguel, I don't think I can help. I really can't go to America right now."

"Oh, no, I don't want you to go to America. She has to be here in Spain. Let me tell you my story."

The Story

"When I was eighteen and my sister Teresa was fourteen I left and went to America. This was sixty-four years ago. I wrote to my parents and Teresa and they wrote to me for several years. After about four years my letters to them started to be returned. I stopped getting mail from them. I did not understand, at least not until I returned here and learned that the home I had lived in with my parents had burned and my parents had burned also. I learned that Teresa had not been in the house when it burned to the ground. This was sixty-nine years ago. No one form the old neighborhood knows where Teresa went or what happened to her. She may not have had my address to write to me since the fire destroyed everything. She was eighteen at the time so she didn't have to go to a foster home or orphanage. I have found out that she married a man name Garcia Godinez. I know he was killed in an accident at a construction job where he worked. This was about six years after they were married. They did not have any children. I haven't been able to find out what she did or where she went after her husband died. She was in Salamanca at that time. I came here about eight months ago and I have been searching and now I have run up against a wall and don't know what to do. I've come to you because I am tired and I can't think of what more I can do. Will you try to find my sister?"

Valdes, thought about it and he felt compassion for Juan Miguel. He didn't have any pressing jobs right then, so he agreed to try to find his sister.

Valdes looked at his watch and said, "It's lunch time. How about we go eat lunch and we will talk some more while we eat."

While they were eating, Valdes was telling Juan about the gatos at the nursing residencia, and how they had made a big change in the lives of the patients who lived there. Juan said, "I would certainly like to see these gatos. I have always had a great fondness for gatos. If you are not too busy, could you take me to see them after we finish our lunch?"

Valdes said, "Yes we can go there and while we are there I would like you to meet the head nurse, whom I am very fond of." Then he kind of chuckled.

Juan told Valdes how he had arrived in America and had got a job, worked hard and saved his money. How one day he thought of how something could be done a lot easier and a lot cheaper. He quit his job and took the money he had been saving, made a model of his idea and got a patent on it. He then went to the manufacturer and sold it to them for a great sum of money plus royalties. It became so popular that he had made millions of dollars over the years. He had married and they had a son and life was good, until about five years ago, when his wife and son were killed in an auto accident. After a mourning period he began to think about his family back in Spain. That is when he began to try to find out what happened to his family. He hired many private investigators but none of them were able to find anything, if they even tried. He became more and more obsessed with finding what had happened to his family. About a year ago he finally decided he would come home to Spain. He sold his home and everything packed his bags and came back eight months ago to see what he could find himself.

After lunch they went to the residencia. Juan was delighted with the gato family and laughed about how the gatos put, not one, but two, things over on the nurses. He especially enjoyed the story about Sookie sneaking the flowers to the patients. He saw how much Valdes thought of Nurse Concha and how much she liked him. He thought they are in love with each other.

Juan saw how happy and contented the elderly patients were and felt a little envy. He met Dr. Mark and later told Valdes, "What a nice young man that Dr. Mark is."

Later that evening, Valdes took Concha to dinner. They were discussing their day and the patients and the gatos. Valdes was telling Concha about Juan hiring him to find his sister.

He mentioned the few facts Juan had given him. Something that Valdes said nagged at her mind but she couldn't quite decide what it was.

Several days later Juan was in Valdes office and he asked if Valdes would draw up a will for him. Valdes suggested he might want to wait awhile to see if his sister could be found. It might make a difference in how he wanted his will.

Juan said maybe he was right about the will. "What I really want is to give some money away to a good cause. I was thinking after our visit to the hospital, that they looked like they could use some money to buy some new equipment and other things they need. Can you handle this for me?"

"How much money are we talking about," asked Valdes.

"Oh, about three million or more," answered Juan. "Unless I find my sister, I don't have any family to leave it to. If I do find Teresa, there is more money coming in all the time."

"Wow!" said Valdes, "they could sure put that kind of money to good use. I would be glad to handle that for you. Where are you staying? I'll need some information."

Juan said, "Well there's that too—I believe I would like to stay at the residencia, I'm getting old, and finding it difficult getting around, and I find I forget to take my medicine too often. Do you think they might find room for me?"

Valdes picked up the phone and dialed, while he said, "Let's find out." Nurse Concha answered the phone and after listening to

Valdes, she said she would call him back as soon as she checked.

When Concha asked Dr. Mark, after explaining, he said, he was sure it would be all right.

He said, "We can use Jose's room since it's empty. Tell Valdes to give us two or three days to clean and repaint and get the room ready, then Mr. Miguel can move in."

Concha called Valdes back and she told him, "I talked to Dr. Mark and asked him if Mr. Miguel could be admitted as a patient to the nursing residencia and he agreed, but asked for three days to clean and paint and get the room ready."

Since Juan was still in the office, Valdes told him that he could move into the residencia in three days.

Meanwhile Valdes was very busy with the two new jobs, which Juan had given him. He was meeting with Juan daily getting information about the donation he was giving to the hospital and also trying to get more information about Juan's sister.

When the room at the residencia was ready, Valdes escorted Juan and his luggage to the hospital where Juan was shown to his room. Valdes had sent flowers to be put in his room and Concha had bought a bright new spread to make the room cheerful and comfortable. Juan, said, "How nice everything looks. I know I will be happy here."

Sister Delores had come in about that time and she offered to take Juan around and show him where everything was located. Delores and Juan left.

Valdes and Concha, left alone, looked at each other and Valdes moved close. He leaned over without touching her and gave her a light kiss with only their lips touching.

He said, "Will you have dinner with me tonight?"

"Yes," she said "seven o'clock."

He said, "I'll pick you up at your apartment at seven." He turned and left.

Concha felt happy and light hearted for the rest of the afternoon thinking about the kiss and spending the evening with Valdes.

Sister Delores showed Juan the day room where patients sat and relaxed when it was too cool to sit on the patio, which was their favorite place. Next they went to the dining room where Juan was introduced to the cook, who asked Juan if he was allergic to any foods. Juan said, "I don't like carrots but I'm not allergic to them." Then he gave a little laugh, which Sister Delores and the cook joined in. They stopped at the nursing station and Sister pointed out Dr. Mark's office and head nurse Concha's office. From there they went out onto the patio and from there she pointed to the path leading to the flower garden and the washhouse where the gatos slept at night. Juan thought the gatos should have a place of their own. He would talk to Valdes about that. As they were making their tour of the residencia they met some of the patients. Sister introduced the patients to Juan. Several patients were in their rooms so they were not disturbed. When Juan returned to his room he laid down to rest. He dozed for about an hour and a half. A tap on his door awakened him. It was head nurse Concha asking how he was.

He answered, "I am fine. I just took a short nap."

Concha said, "Would you like to meet the other patients?"

Juan answered, "Sister introduced me to several, when she was showing me around this morning. I did not meet everyone, so I would like to meet the rest. Let me get a drink of water and smooth my hair and I'll be ready in a jiffy."

Concha nodded an okay.

Juan and Concha headed for the day room where some of the patients were sitting and waiting for lunch to be ready. Concha went around and introduced each patient to Juan. Some said that they had met him earlier and they spoke to Juan again.

Teresa was sitting by herself in an old armchair. Concha took Juan by his arm and pulled him closer, because Teresa had trouble seeing. She introduced Juan, "Teresa, this is Juan, Juan this is Teresa."

"I have a brother named Juan," Teresa said. "I haven't seen him in a long, long time. He may not even be alive any more."

Juan took her hand and said, "Isn't that a coincidence? I have a sister named Teresa, whom I haven't seen or heard from in many years."

Teresa asked, "What is your last name, Juan?"

"Miguel," Juan said.

Concha groaned, "Oh my goodness! Teresa, what was your maiden name?"

"Miguel," Teresa whispered, "did you go to America when you were eighteen?"

"Yes," Juan answered. "I believe you are my little sister that I have been searching for. I wrote, and my letters kept being returned. I didn't know until a few months ago that our parents died in the fire when our home burned down. No one could tell me anything about you, except that you were not at home when the house burned. No one knew where you went. I found that you had married a man named Godinez, but he died. After that I wasn't able to discover anymore."

"I remarried, A Dominguez, he died about eight years ago. I never had any niños. You are my brother." Teresa got up from the chair and Juan hugged her and they both cried, because they were so happy. Concha cried too.

The lunch bell rang and they went into lunch hand in hand. They had sixty years of catching up to do.

Mattie and Oliver get married

Mattie woke up extra early on the thirtieth. It was her wedding day. She was so excited. Sister Barbara came in and helped her with her bath and Mattie decided to go into breakfast in her robe. Her daughters would be coming soon to help her get ready for the wedding. It was to be at ten o'clock. While she was still in the dining room eating, her two daughters arrived. They got themselves cups of coffee and they all sat and visited while Mattie finished her breakfast. Mattie's oldest daughter asked her, "Mama, are you ready to do this?"

Mattie looked at her daughters and told them, "I really love Oliver, and I don't want to spend the rest of my life alone. God sent me Oliver he loves me. We want to be married. I will make him happy and he will make me happy. Now I'm finished. Are you both finished with your coffee? Let's go back to my room so I can get ready for my wedding."

Dr. Mark was to be best man for his grandfather, Oliver. A little before ten o'clock Mark and his grandfather arrived at the chapel to find the chaplain already there.

Ferns and white flowers in baskets were at each side of a tall candelabrum holding twelve white candles. Mattie's oldest grandson lit the candles. The chapel was about half full with Mattie's family and the residencia patients and some of their families who had been at the birthday party the month before. The nurses and Dr. Sainz were present also.

Mattie was escorted down the aisle by her two sons, one on each side. Oliver, waiting as she came forward towards him, thought she was so lovely as she walked with her skirt swirling around her. He was so happy she was marrying him. His son, Mark's father and Mark's mother were there and they were happy for him.

Soon, the chaplain announced Mattie and Oliver as man and wife. The chaplain said, "I present to you, Mr. and Mrs. Tapia."

Everyone clapped.

There was wine and wedding cake afterwards in the dining room, and sandwiches for those who wanted them.

The new married couple did not plan to go on a wedding trip.

Oliver's son and daughter-in-law were going to take them out to a fancy restaurant later in the evening, after Mark and Connie's wedding and after they left on their honeymoon.

Dr. Mark and Nurse Connie's Wedding

Connie's family arrived while Mattie and Oliver were being married. They had never met Dr. Mark but he planned to meet them after his grandfather's wedding. He stopped by their hotel on his way back to his apartment to change clothes for his wedding. He had worn a navy suit to stand up for his grandfather, and he was going to wear a tuxedo for his own wedding.

Later, Connie's mother and grandmother told her that they had talked to Mark and they liked him very much. Her father had liked him also. They were pleased and thought Connie had made a good choice.

After talking to Mark, her mother and grandmother went to Connie's apartment to help her get ready. She had everything there except the flowers, which were to be delivered to the hospital. Nurse Concha was to be Connie's maid of honor. Her dress was pink chiffon and she was to carry two long stem pink rose buds.

They were going to have only the two attendants, Best man and Maid of Honor, since they were getting married so quickly. They were so busy at the hospital they didn't have much time to plan a large wedding. Besides that, they wanted to get married in the hospital chapel so the patients and nurses and doctors could attend the wedding. They had arranged to take a week off to have a honeymoon.

Mark arrived back at the hospital at one-thirty, with his father, who was his best man. The nosegay, which Connie was to carry, was there as well as the corsages for her mother, grandmother and Mark's mother and new grandmother, Mattie. The boutonnieres for the men were tiny white rose buds with the corsages for the women being pink rosebuds.

When Connie's father escorted her down the aisle he whispered to her, just before thy started, "I approve of you choice of a husband. He seems to be a good person. I love you daughter and I'm proud of you. Be happy."

She whispered back, "I will be, I love you too, Daddy."

Dr. Mark watched, as Connie and her father walked down the aisle. Love for her swelled up in his heart and he vowed to love her and care for her for the rest of his life.

Soon the wedding was over, the pictures taken and everyone went into the day room where the big wedding cake was cut. Wine was served as well as hors d'oeuvres, canapés and dips, nut, crackers and mints and cheese and olives.

Finally Dr. Mark and Connie were ready to leave. Connie threw her nosegay and Concha caught it. Connie laughed, "It looks like you will be the next bride." Concha blushed and Valdes laughed too because he hoped it was true. He intended to see that it would become true.

Rice was thrown on the couple as they run for the coche, to leave on their wedding trip.

The guests left. Mattie and Oliver left with his son and daughter-in-law to have dinner at a restaurant and the residencia patients were ready to get settled in their rooms for the night.

As Concha went back to her office she wondered what her future would bring. She knew that she loved Valdes but he had not said how he felt about her.

Valdes planned to tell her that her future was with him, very soon.

Epilogue

Several days later, Juan called Valdes and asked him if he could come by the residencia. When Valdes arrived, Juan said, "I've been thinking about the gatos, they have done so much for the patients here, I think we need to do something for them. I want to have a small building that's suitable for them, so they won't have to sleep in the washhouse. I also want to know if you have the check for the donation to the hospital ready yet."

Valdes said, "The money has been transferred from your bank in America to the bank here in Salamanca. There is more than enough to donate three and a half million to the hospital. Do you want to specify how it is to be used?"

Juan said, "Let's make three million dollars with no strings attached and the other half million to be used to redecorate the patients rooms in the residencia. The day room needs new rugs and drapes. It could also use some new comfortable chairs and sofas and a writing desk, new lamps and a very big screen T.V.

"Okay," said Valdes "consider it done. I'll have the paper work and the check for the three million dollars ready for you in a couple of days and then we will get started on the gatos house and the improvements on the residencia."

Valdes stopped by Concha's office and closed the door. He asked Concha if she was ready for another wedding.

Concha said, "Oh, no, who is it this time?"

Valdes grinned, "I was hoping it would be you and me. I love you and I want you to be my wife and spend the rest of our lives with each other. Will you marry me?"

"I love you too Valdes and I will marry you, but let's wait a couple of months before we get married."

"Whatever you want," said Valdes as he gathered her in his arms and kissed her.

Flor lay watching on the windowsill, with satisfaction and pride. She went to tell the gato family what they had accomplished for their people.

Spanish	English
Gatos	Cats
Blanco	White
Negro	Black
Muy grande	Very large
Calle	Street
Padre	Father
Coche	Car
Flor	Flower
Dos	Two
Doce	Twelve
Senors	Men
Senoras	Ladies
Seis	Six
Anciano la gente	Old people
La muchacha gatos	Girl cats
Hablo	Talk
Buenas dias	Good morning

Bebe	Baby
Poco	Little
Hijos	Sons
Hijas	Daughters
Café	Coffee
Avenida	Avenue

Beverley B. Starr

About the Author

Retiring after seven years as an artist for the Marine Corps Supply Center, Beverley enrolled in college to study art. After two years at Darton College and two years at Albany State University, she received a B.S. degree in Art in 1985 at the age of fifty-seven. Soon after this she participated in the International Intercultural Studies Program of the University System of Georgia, on an eight-week trip to Salamanca, Spain. This book resulted from experiences she had there She has three children and eight grandchildren and three great grandchildren. She resides in Albany, Georgia with her loving cat, Misty.